For Audrey, who asked, "I wonder where food banks came from."
— J.G.

This book is for my little sister, Ariel, the brilliant aspiring chef.
— M.L.A.

Library of Congress Control Number: 2022945648

Published by Creston Books, LLC
www.crestonbooks.co

ISBN 978-1-954354-24-1
Source of Production: 1010 Printing
Printed and bound in China
5 4 3 2 1

Food For Hope

By Jeff Gottesfeld

Illustrated by Michelle Laurentia Agatha

"The poor we shall always have with us, but why the hungry?"

— John van Hengel, inspired by John 12:8

The cruel Arizona sun beat down on a ragged line of people that snaked away from a church door. John van Hengel was in that line.

The wait was long and hot, but worth it. Inside was a dining room for the needy. The menu was boring — soup, rice and beans, powdered milk — but it was the difference between an empty stomach and being fed. John knew the mind-numbing ache of hunger. So did everyone there. They were grateful for the free meal.

In faraway Waupun, Wisconsin, where John was born, few would ever have imagined him in a soup line. He seemed to have been born lucky. His mother was a nurse, and his dad owned a drugstore with an ice cream counter. He grew up to be handsome and athletic. After college, he went to California to play tennis with movie stars. A born salesman, money rolled in. He married, had two sons, and bought a home near the ocean.

Then his luck ran out. He lost everything. For the first time in his life, John worried about his next meal. And the next. And the next.

John liked people. He talked with everyone in the dining room — disabled veterans, the homeless, and kids whose parents had to choose between rent and food. Their stories opened his heart. He found work at the kitchen, shelter in a cheap room above a garage, and faith in prayer with Father Ronald at St. Mary's Church.

With his simple life, John was no longer hungry. But it was not like his kitchen fed people well. He heard kids clamor for fresh fruit and remembered the citrus orchards east of town. He drove out in a battered pickup truck and convinced the growers to let a volunteer crew harvest grapefruit that would rot on the ground otherwise. They gathered so much extra that John drove it to other charities.

It was a joy to see everyone enjoy the fruit. John wanted to feed more people. He just didn't know how.

During one grapefruit delivery, he heard an unemployed mother boast that she got food at a special store. Her kids ate like the rich, for free. John thought she was making it up, until the woman practically dragged him to a supermarket dumpster. "Look!" she ordered.

John peered inside. The bin overflowed with banged-up cans, crushed boxes of dry goods, and piles of bruised but edible vegetables. This was her "store." She was only sorry she couldn't put the extra in a bank. John never got her name but always gave her credit. He rushed to St. Mary's, excited by the possibilities.

"We need a food bank!" he exclaimed. "A place to share food that's being thrown out."

"It's a great idea," Father Ronald agreed. "Do it."

"Hold on," John protested. "I already cook at the mission. My plate is full!"

The priest smiled. "You heard the call, John. Decide if you want to listen."

Six months later, John opened the St. Mary's Food Bank in an abandoned bakery. He scrawled a quote from the Gospels on a board above his rickety desk, adding his own twist:

"The poor we shall always have with us, but why the hungry?"

John needed a lot of food to help the needy of his community. He found it in supermarket warehouses. He looked like a beggar, but his message to the managers was powerful: Don't discard what you can't sell. Give it to the hungry.

Donations rolled in.
Cases of dented canned anchovies.

Boxes of broken spaghetti.
And one memorable day, 5,000 squawking chickens.

St. Mary's distributed 125 tons of food to kitchens and food pantries the very first year. It ran on volunteer labor. To John's delight, his grownup sons came to help him. They found takers for everything.

Even the chickens.

A government agency offered money to spread the idea. John didn't want to change his humble life. He just wanted to feed more people. He named the new charity "Second Harvest" but never accepted a paycheck. It opened dozens of food banks across America. More food arrived than he could ever imagine.

37 railroad cars of discontinued cereal.
2 million bottles of discolored juice.
17 trailers of frozen trout.
And on another memorable day,
a million chocolate Easter bunnies.

Smiling volunteers found takers for everything.

Even the bunnies

John traveled the world to open food banks but never forgot those being fed. He worked to the end, and talked to young and old at dining rooms and pantries. When a first grader heard that the frail man sitting on the bench in thrift store clothes and white–painted shoes was the father of food banking, he shook John's trembling hand. "You did good," he said.

That is food for hope.

Author's Note

I came to John van Hengel's story in an unlikely fashion. My stepdaughter Audrey must have been in eighth grade when we were batting around book ideas. She was a volunteer at the North Hollywood (CA) Interfaith Food Pantry, and asked, "Well, maybe here's an idea. Who invented food banks, anyway?"

The answer to that question is this book. The deeper I got into the subject, the more compelling it was. I loved that John van Hengel grew up anything but hungry. He had a middle-class upbringing in small town Waupun, Wisconsin. Smart, athletic, and charismatic, van Hengel earned the nickname "Doc" in high school and was elected class president. After studying government at Lawrence University in Appleton, WI, he headed to California to seek his fortune. Soon he was a well-paid corporate vice president. By the late 1950s, with a home near the ocean in Ventura, CA, a wife who was a former model, and their two sons, his life seemed like the American dream come true.

I loved that the story is riches-to-rags, instead of rags-to-riches. Unexpectedly, van Hengel's life fell apart. His wife divorced him. His boys stayed with their mother. He lost his job. As he told the Los Angeles Times, "I took off back to Wisconsin, hurt, escaping, and so angry that I wanted the worst job I could find."

Van Hengel went from bad to worse. One day, he broke up a fight between two coworkers and was so badly hurt that he needed neurosurgery. He came out of the operation unable to walk properly. His doctors suggested that the warm, dry weather of Arizona might help him heal. So, with neither a job nor a home awaiting him, van Hengel went to Phoenix.

I loved too that misfortune and renewed religious faith and observance became van Hengel's catalyst for change. In time, his sons visited him in Phoenix, and helped at the food bank. Van Hengel left America's Second Harvest in the early 1980s to spread the good news about food banking and and help establish food banks around the world. He worked until he died of Parkinson's Disease in 2005, self-effacing to the end. His typical response when offered awards for his life work? "You can't eat off a trophy."

I love too that *Food for Hope* can help focus attention on the disheartening subject of food insecurity. Even with Feeding America providing 2 billion pounds of food annually to charities and food banks distributing 5 billion pounds of food overall, an estimated 1 out of 8 Americans suffers from food insecurity, including 13 million children. Around the world, the figures are even more dismal. Life's fortune can change suddenly, like van Hengel's did. There is no shame in being hungry. The shame is in having the capacity to feed everyone, and failing to muster the will to do just that.

John van Hengel's life shows us what is possible, and what a difference one person can make.

Terminology

Food Banks are central repositories for donated food. They may or may not have a public distribution arm themselves. They most often distribute food to social service organizations that run food pantries, where people can pick up the donated food. Soup kitchens and charity dining rooms are places that serve free meals. They often use ingredients that come from food banks or food pantries.

A Note on Research and Dialogue

All dialogue in this book is taken either from published newspaper accounts or from interviews with people who knew John van Hengel. Among those whom the author interviewed were John van Hengel, Jr. (son); Thomas van Hengel (son); Stephen Morris (friend and St. Mary's volunteer); and Jen Tresinski (historian, St. Joseph's Catholic Church, Waupun, WI). I also had assistance from the Waupun Historical Society, and the Arizona Historical Society, which holds the archives of the St. Mary's Food Bank. There are multiple versions of the story about how van Hengel encountered the unnamed woman who gave him the idea for food banking.

Timeline

Feb. 21, 1923:	John van Hengel born, Waupun, WI
1940:	Graduates Waupun High School
1944:	Graduates Lawrence University, Appleton, WI, with degree in government
1945:	Moves to California, marries and has two sons. Becomes vice president of a division of Bear Archery, Inc.
1960:	Divorces, returns to Wisconsin
Circa 1963:	Moves to Arizona
Mid-1960s:	Cooks at St. Vincent de Paul charity kitchen, which was feeding 1,000 people a day. Does other odd jobs
1967:	Meets unknown woman who shows him usable food in a supermarket dumpster
1967:	Founds St. Mary's Food Bank, Phoenix, AZ, in an abandoned bakery donated by St. Mary's Church. Staffed only by van Hengel and a few volunteers, it distributes 250,000 pounds of food to charities the very first year
1968:	CBS television network runs groundbreaking documentary on "Hunger in America." The country awakens to the problem of food insecurity
1975:	Accepts federal grant, opens 18 food banks, and establishes America's Second Harvest
1977:	Food banks in 17 American cities
1983:	Van Hengel leaves Second Harvest to found what would become the Global Food Banking Network, focused on establishing food banks internationally
1992:	Food banks in 200 American cities. Also Canada, France, Belgium, Ireland, United Kingdom, Spain, Italy, Haiti, Ghana, and Sri Lanka
Oct. 5, 2005:	John van Hengel dies of Parkinson's Disease in Phoenix, AZ. He maintains a vow of poverty to his death and is buried in Waupun, WI
2005:	Second Harvest supports 50,000 charitable agencies operating food pantries, soup kitchens, and other programs
2008:	Second Harvest becomes Feeding America
2013:	Food banks now open in Nepal, South Korea, Egypt, China, India, across Central and South America, Malawi and Japan
2018:	Global Food Banking Network has 811 food banks in its international network, serving 55,013 agencies.
Today:	In the United States alone, there are 200 Feeding America food banks, plus many others, and 60,000+ food pantries and programs